Dea Coschignano, Ph.D.

Treatment Manual for Post Traumatic Stress Disorder

BALBOA.PRESS
A DIVISION OF HAY HOUSE

Balboa Press books may be ordered through booksellers or by contacting:

Balboa Press
A Division of Hay House
1663 Liberty Drive
Bloomington, IN 47403
www.balboapress.com
844-682-1282

Because of the dynamic nature of the Internet, any web addresses or links contained in this book may have changed since publication and may no longer be valid. The views expressed in this work are solely those of the author and do not necessarily reflect the views of the publisher, and the publisher hereby disclaims any responsibility for them.

The author of this book does not dispense medical advice or prescribe the use of any technique as a form of treatment for physical, emotional, or medical problems without the advice of a physician, either directly or indirectly. The intent of the author is only to offer information of a general nature to help you in your quest for emotional and spiritual well-being. In the event you use any of the information in this book for yourself, which is your constitutional right, the author and the publisher assume no responsibility for your actions.

Any people depicted in stock imagery provided by Getty Images are models, and such images are being used for illustrative purposes only.
Certain stock imagery © Getty Images.

ISBN: 978-1-9822-5948-8 (sc)
ISBN: 978-1-9822-5955-6 (e)

Library of Congress Control Number: 2020923450

Print information available on the last page.

Balboa Press rev. date: 11/24/2020

C O N T E N T S

ABOUT THE AUTHOR

Dr. Dea Coschignano has worked as a licensed psychologist in Colorado and Hawaii. She earned her Ph.D. in Psychology in 2000 and has specialized in treating trauma -- all kinds of trauma, from soldiers who were deployed to Iraq and Afghanistan to those injured in car accidents, as well as victims of sexual abuse and assault. She uses EMDR (Eye Movement Desensitization and Reprocessing) a very effective trauma treatment as well as teaching coping skills such as DBT and Meditation. She is aware of the current research in the field including Neuropsychological research on the benefits of meditation for the brain. Her book provides the basics in trauma treatment for providers and patients as well. She worked in Fort Carson with active duty Army soldiers for 3 years and in the outer islands of Hawaii for 6 years doing social security disability assessments. You will find her entertaining and enlightening about surviving trauma and having a new life as you recover or help your clients to recover.

PREFACE

Posttraumatic stress disorder, and culture are my two main interests. I have worked with car accident victims, active duty Army soldiers at Fort Carson, Colorado, who had been in Iraq and Afghanistan, as well as with domestic violence victims, and adults and children with sexual abuse and rape histories. Most recently I have been doing social security disability assessments and see those traumatized by car accidents and illnesses. So, for 24 years I have been putting together treatments from some of the best people in the field and decided it was time to share what I have learned with those just coming into the treatment field, or in school studying to become providers, or with those working on their own treatment. I have found this work exciting and very rewarding and I hope this Manuel is helpful to you as you embark on your career or treatment and healing journey.

My graduate studies for the Ph.D. was with Saybrook University now Oakland, California so I come from a body-mind-spirit approach to healing. Saybrook was founded by Rollo May, one of the humanistic psychologists. Maslow, another of the humanistic psychologists, thought we should be studying the healthy for inspiration about how to heal the sick. I will share what I consider some of the most inspirational authors, healers, and healing techniques in these pages; techniques I have used in treating PTSD; and, some aspects of the experiences and healing journeys of some victims. My treatment approach is three fold, including body, mind, and spirit. If you are new to work with trauma, or trying to heal yourself from PTSD, this book provides guidance and suggestions about what works and the best healing techniques for all types of traumas whatever their source. An excellent book, <u>When the Body Says No: Exploring the Stress-Disease Connection</u> (2003) by Dr. Mate explores the personal histories of his patients. He found those with early abuse often were more likely to develop physical ailments later in their lives. I have discovered the same thing in my work with patients, specifically in the disability assessments I have done with thousands of patients in the last few years. Early abuse or neglect, which can produce PTSD symptoms, seems to have a long-lasting effect when not addressed, and, may be a precursor to severe physical health problems later in life.

CHAPTER 1

UNDERSTANDING TRAUMA

Frank Bruni in an article titled "What War Means" in the September 15, 2013 New York Times reported that, "Our country sent more than two million men and women to fight in Iraq and Afghanistan. More than 6,500 of them are dead. Tens of thousands were physically injured, including 1,500 amputees... Then he quotes author David Finkel in his book released in October 2013 titled, Thank You For Your Service, regarding those with PTSD. Finkel says, "Of the two-million-plus Americans who spent time there [in Iraq or Afghanistan], studies suggest 20 to 30 percent have come home with posttraumatic stress disorder. (New York Times, September 15, 2013, Sunday Review, p. 3).

For 3 years, I worked with soldiers at the Evans Army Community Hospital in Fort Carson, Colorado working with active duty soldiers, many who had been deployed to Iraq and Afghanistan. I learned a tremendous amount working with them. We performed triage -- soldiers in distress came in and we provided therapy, and, if necessary, we hospitalized them. I coordinated work with their primary care physicians. Many soldiers had physical injuries as well as mental health problems

The soldiers I worked with had often come face to face with death; if not themselves, then the death of those who were very dear to them, their buddies who "had their backs." Many soldiers expressed a fatalistic belief regarding life and death on the battlefield saying, "when your number's up your number's up." They had great loyalty to those who never came home and often wore metal bracelets identifying the names of their buddies; called their buddies' families; and, swore never to forget them. Working with soldiers was, for me, working with the dedicated and well disciplined. I loved working with the soldiers. They had given their all, for us, and deserved our compassion and the best of our healing skills. The 3 years working with them was a wonderful experience.

I have now worked in the field of trauma for many years with soldiers returning from Iraq and Afghanistan, with battered women in domestic violence situations, and with rape victims and sexually abused children. PTSD (Posttraumatic Stress Disorder) is common to all these experiences. As with AA and alcoholism it is often helpful to rely on your higher power or spiritual and religious beliefs to help you through the many difficulties that are encountered as you work toward healing. This is the spiritual part of the body-mind spirit approach to treatment.

It seems that multiple traumas are the norm. The reason for this is, in my experience, many individuals have complicated lives that involve a history of several different traumas from different sources and from different time periods. For example, you are a soldier with several deployments that were difficult and you have been diagnosed with PTSD, and as you are dealing with this issue, you are reminded of the abuse in your childhood or adolescence. Or, you are a female soldier and are raped while deployed, and, all of a sudden you begin to remember and have flashbacks about sexual abuse in childhood or a rape that occurred in your earlier life. Sometimes things just pile up. And, we begin to realize that we have been carrying these issues around for years. When another trauma is added to the pile we have to face them all. It is as if the current trauma ignites all those we have not dealt with from our past.

Trauma victims may find it mysterious and inexplicable that, just a few months before, they were feeling fine. They may have forgotten, and buried all those issues from their younger years. They may ask, "Why is it bothering me now?" New traumas often awaken earlier traumas. All of a sudden everything comes up at once and we can no longer avoid dealing with it all. Sometimes the old traumas have been ignored because we were not yet strong enough to deal with them. We had to become more mature and allow some distance from them so they would not overwhelm us. It seems that the mind protects us signaling when we are strong enough to do the work of healing. If past issues are coming up now then now is the time to deal with them.

Re-entry After Deployment – Coming Home

Soldiers may also have difficulty adjusting when they return to the U.S. Sometimes it can be harder coming home than deploying. Service

Members often find the re-entry process occurs in stages. Their body is here but their mind is still in Iraq or Afghanistan, at least part of the time. They have been exposed to a totally different culture, made friends with, and often worked next to individuals from these foreign cultures. They may have tried their foods, learned about their culture, enjoyed their children and families, learned some of their language, and, felt like they were there to help. They have lived through a culture shock experience made more intense because it was under conditions of war. They may now consider themselves citizens of the world. After seeing hungry, poor, Iraqis and Afghanis, they may view the general public in the U.S. with new eyes. They may either be very happy to be home and not miss deployment at all, or actually miss being deployed since they can often feel more appreciated by their Chain of Command when in the war zone than back at the Post. Their work while deployed is often rewarded with increased rank, and financial remuneration -- more money to pay off the bills or buy a new car or home. Perhaps their Unit may have deployed again, or some of their battle buddies have deployed again, and they wish they were with them and are worried about them. Coming home is a complicated business, different for every service member, because, of course, we are all unique.

They also may have witnessed and been a participant in the duties of a warrior – firefights, house searches, convoys, seeing IEDs on the roads and mortars coming into their camp. Fellow soldiers they knew and befriended may have died while serving. They may feel like it is their duty not to forget them and their sacrifice. They may have witnessed deaths and cleaned up body parts. These experiences can be hard to forget and deal with.

Talking about their own deployment experience or experiences, telling their story, with all its elements, is vitally important for them. They need a good listener and often it requires a professional with knowledge of post-traumatic stress disorder, who cares about what the soldier went through and who is interested in them and their experience; each soldier's own unique experience. It can take some time for them to feel like they are really home. As they start talking they will discover just how complicated the whole deployment and re-entry to the U.S. can be. Burying the experiences and stuffing the feelings, or trying to drown them with alcohol, is not advised. Although some Service Members may give this approach a try, it does not seem to work, and, unfortunately, may give them another problem -- substance abuse.

There are many methods for dealing with trauma issues, and, I used EMDR, which is evidence based and researched as a very effective treatment, and it can be requested from mental health providers. Go on line and review the information at www.emdr.com.

A lot can change at home over a year's time. Let's be honest, it can be hard to maintain a relationship and family ties and friendships when a soldier is deployed. Of course, many military families have done so and will continue to do so. The soldier's spouse may notice that they have changed. How could they not have? They have just undergone a life-changing experience, either once or several times. Even those who live abroad for school, the Peace Corp, or diplomatic stations, find they have changed and their home looks different when they return to it, and, they have lived abroad under peaceful, much easier conditions, than soldiers have. Other stressors can include the injuries service members have sustained, and the need for surgeries and treatment for them, upon their return to the U.S.

If soldiers feel different upon their return to the U.S., they can well imagine their spouses, children, and other friends and relatives, will have grown and changed, as well. Home may feel unfamiliar. It can take time to become reacquainted with family and friends. Many soldiers worry that telling family about their deployment will be bad for family members and they decide not to share much about it. They can feel very different and think, "I'm not the same person I was before I deployed." They may have new physical challenges due to injuries. It is important to learn good self-care now. Relationships may need some adjustments. Excellent techniques for marital therapy can be found in the books of John M. Gottman, Ph.D. listed in Appendix A. He recommends maintaining a strong friendship with one's significant other as the key for long lasting love relationships.

Domestic Violence & Other Traumas

Twenty-five percent of women experience domestic violence and sexual abuse. One in every 4 females and one in every 6 males experience rape or sexual abuse in their life times.

We have become, as a society, much more open about discussing domestic violence and sexual abuse issues. There are domestic violence 24-hour hot lines and shelters in most large communities. In the 1990s I was privileged to attend a 2-week training on domestic violence at Boulder County Safehouse before working as a counselor there. I also attended countless trainings on sexual abuse in preparation for work with victims and perpetrators, from the experts in the field: Jan Hindman, Ph.D., author of, <u>Just Before Dawn: From the Shadows of Tradition to New Reflections in Trauma Assessment and Treatment of Sexual Victimization</u> (1989); and, John Briere, Ph.D. author of <u>Therapy for Adults Molested as Children: Beyond Survival</u> (1989) and others. Here are some of the most important things for those with this experience to know:

- Do not hesitate to call the National Domestic Violence Hotline for a listing of the shelters near you at 1-800-799-7233.
- If you are looking for information on domestic violence call the National Coalition Against Domestic Violence at (303) 839-1852.
- For soldiers, call military one source for help at 1-800-342-9647.
- Your experience or experiences will start changing and becoming less toxic the minute you find a well-trained person to talk to and help you work through them.
- I recommend EMDR as a great treatment. (See the website www.emdr.com website to find a trained therapist in your area).
- Remember, trauma is a common issue for many, many people. Now that it is out in the open the chances for healing from it have multiplied many times from where it was in the 1950s and earlier.
- Believe it or not, some day this issue will not have the charge that it has now for you, before you have addressed it. You will get over it and be able to put it behind you.
- If you have many other traumas, such as deployments, divorce, sexual abuse as a child and then a rape in adulthood, the pressure to work on these issues will increase. It does not matter how many traumas you have, they can all be healed, one at a time. I have worked with soldiers who have deployment trauma, sexual abuse in childhood and rape in their adult years, and they have healed well. I have also worked with domestic violence victims who have had multiple traumas. They have healed. So can you. Just know you are not alone. The world is full of people who have these issues.

Victims of rape, sexual and physical abuse and neglect can have some complicated relationships to deal with. Intra-familial abuse is between family members. Extra-familial abuse is between non-family members. The later is generally easier to deal with. If you are dealing with intra-familial abuse, your genetic heritage may have these issues that go way back. You then are the one that will bring healing to the family and future generations, by your courage in dealing with this difficult issue and your resolve in not passing it on to the next generation.

When the abuse you went through is from a family member there is the whole network of relatives to deal with, which can complicate things a little or a lot. Sometimes, a time out from these relationships is advised, so that you can heal in peace. I don't recommend confronting them; which can cause a lot of conflict and be difficult for you; but, working on changing the relationship is important so that it meets your needs now, not just theirs. Age is also a key issue in the healing process. Some enlightened communities, intervene in intra-familial and extra-familial cases that involve children and adolescents, but, as I have discovered, in working with soldiers from around the country, with these issues that date back to their childhoods, many communities do not intervene.

By far the biggest and most difficult issue for those who have suffered abuse in their childhood and adolescence is to realize that they were never at fault. The adult or older perpetrator is the one who bears responsibility. Absorbing and accepting this truth often contradicts everything the perpetrator has said over and over to the victim. A perpetrator will first try to "groom" a victim, choosing someone who is more vulnerable due to difficult family circumstances, and then provide warmth and presents, along with warnings that if the victim should tell, something dire will happen. So, recovering and healing from this sort of abuse requires that the victim become familiar with the criminal ways of perpetrators; the way they shift blame off their shoulders onto yours. Healing requires that you shift the blame back where it belongs. Domestic violence victims can have the same tactics used against them by their perpetrators. In addition to leaving and finding safety, they often have to deal with several children, finances, and multiple other concerns.

All this is easier with extra-familial abuse, if the offender is a parent, or spouse, the internal conflict may be much harder. It can often be true that offenders have experienced similar abuse themselves in their own childhoods -- you may be at the end of a long generational curse. Perhaps your husband was a witness of domestic violence growing up. Once you recover your own strength and work through the confusing thoughts such abuse brings, you can decide where you stand with this spouse or parent. You may have already made space or moved away from them. It is up to you to decide what is healthy for you and whom you want to spend time with. The ball is in your court now. You are an adult and as you respect your own feelings, you will make wise decisions that start you off toward a healthier life.

CHAPTER 2

ASSESSMENT

The Army's PTSD Testing Instrument

My work at Fort Carson and with the Boulder County Safehouse was some of the most rewarding of my life. I will share some of what the soldiers and domestic violence victims taught me with you from their experiences. Hopefully, it will help with an understanding of the soldiers who fight for us, and what they are going through, and, what women experience in healing from domestic violence. The following are some of the symptoms of PTSD as described by Weathers, Litz, Huska & Keane (1994). This instrument is used by the Army to test PTSD.

A strong startle response

Feelings of super alertness or hyper-vigilance

Problems with concentration

Having irritability or outbursts of anger

Problems falling or staying asleep

Thoughts that you will not live to an old age

Feeling emotionally numb

Feeling emotionally cut off from others

Having a loss of interest in things you once enjoyed

Memory problems regarding stressful military [or other traumatizing experiences]

Avoiding thinking or talking about stressful military [or other traumatizing] experiences

Avoiding all reminders of stressful military [or other traumatizing] experiences

Physical reactions – heart pounding, trouble breathing, etc.

Flash backs – like stressful military [or other traumatizing] experiences were happening again

Dreams about stressful military [or other traumatizing] experiences

Having recurring thoughts and memories about stressful military [or other traumatizing] experiences.

Beck BAI Anxiety Inventory & BDI-II Depression Inventory

It is good to get a baseline assessment of your anxiety, depression, and posttraumatic stress disorder levels. Psychologists use the BAI, The Beck Anxiety Inventory instrument developed by Aaron T. Beck (1993) and the BDI-II, The Beck Depression Inventory developed by Aaron T. Beck, Robert A. Steer and Gregory K. Brown (1996). Both are available through PsychCorp.com. And, the TSI, The Trauma Symptom Inventory) (1991), a 100 question inventory on Posttraumatic Stress Disorder developed by John Briere, Ph.D. is available through www.parinc.com.

Another good instrument is the test to determine if you are a highly sensitive individual and it can be found in the book, The Highly Sensitive Person's Workbook, Aaron, (1999). If you purchase the book, you can give yourself the test and read the material, which is designed to help you deal with your sensitivity. Any materials on relaxation skills are also helpful, as is bodywork, including acupuncture and massage.

Information from the PTSD Diagnosis from the DSM-5

It is not possible to provide the full diagnosis for PTSD from the DSM-5 but we can give you some details. To be diagnosed with PTSD the patient would have had to experience serious injury, or violence, directly, witnessed it, or heard a family member or friend had gone through it. As a result, the patient would have scary memories, nightmares, or dreams. And, if they were first responders they would have witnessed or heard about such events.

Victims often dissociate, have flashbacks, and in severe cases are not able to keep a dual awareness of where they are at the present time but get lost in their flashback. They can have severe distress as they experience triggers that remind them of the abuse and try to avoid anything that reminds them of it. They can also have loss of memory about the event. Victims can also have trouble experiencing positive feelings, be constantly on guard and believe they will not recover from the events. They can lose interest in activities and people that used to be important to them. Cognitive issues such as memory, focusing and concentration can become difficult. If you wish to read the full Posttraumatic Stress Disorder diagnosis check Pp. 143 – 146, (2013) Desk Reference to the Diagnostic Criteria from DSM-5).

EMDR Patients Can Do Themselves -- Tapping

With the therapy I have done with car accident victims, phone therapy is often used so they can avoid driving. And, due to the Corona Virus, phone and on-line therapy is now very common. I teach Tapping, a form of EMDR, over the phone by instructing patients to put their feet flat on the floor, their hands on your knees and then to tap one knee and then the other knee, back and forth while using positive self-talk --"Everything is going to be fine," "I am feeling better every day," "I am getting stronger." The feedback on Tapping has been very positive.

Waterfall Meditation

Along with the instruction for Tapping, I also teach The Waterfall Meditation via phone. I ask patients to breath deeply, visualize a waterfall, and focus on it. When their

Dea Coschignano, Ph.D.

attention wanders I ask them to keep returning it back to focusing on the Waterfall. Recent neuropsychological research has confirmed Meditation benefits the brain in many ways and my car accident patients find it very relaxing.

Assessment for Patient/Provider

The following assessment interview is based on the DSM-5 diagnosis listed on the previous 2 pages.

1. **What do you consider your strengths?**

_____

_____

2. **How Resilient Are You?**

a) *How do you handle change?*_____

_____

b) *What opportunities have you noticed in recent changes in your life?*

_____

_____

c) *How are you staying healthy?*_____

_____

_____

d) *Have you come up with new ways to handle your work life?*

_____

_____

e) *How are you handling stress?*_____

_____

_____

3. **PTSD Symptoms**

a) *Startle Response: List the times you have reactions to things like: someone coming up behind you without warning; loud noises; and, other events that make you jump or feel stressed.*

_____

_____

_____

_____

Rate how difficult this is for you, anywhere from 10 Very difficult to 1 Easy:

b) *Super Alertness: List the times you have felt on edge, especially aware of and worried about danger, or having trouble sleeping due to worry.*

_____

_____

_____

_____

_____

Rate how difficult this is for you anywhere from 10 very difficult to 1 easy:

c) *Problems Regarding Concentration: List the times it is difficult for you to concentrate. Are you able to drive, balance your checkbook, listen and remember what others say to you? Remember you can always carry a memory aid like a notebook.*

_____

_____

_____

_____

Rate how difficult this is for you, from 10 Very Hard to 1 Easy:

d) *Irritability and Angry Outbursts: How often and under what circumstances do you become irritable and angry? What brings on these reactions? Have you gotten in trouble with the law or into fights? Please list them below.*

_____

_____

_____

_____

_____

_____

Please rate how severe this problem is for you with a score of 10 if very hard to 1 easy:

e) *Sleep: Describe any problems with sleep. Have you had a sleep study? (A study is indicated if you snore loudly or wake up catching your breath). Also indicate how many hours of sleep you get at night on average.*

_____

_____

_____

_____

f) *Shortened Life: Do you have thoughts of a shortened life? Please describe any distress they cause.*

_____

_____

_____

_____

_____

g) *Emotional Numbness: Describe any problems feeling or expressing emotions.*

_____

_____

_____

_____

h) *Are you feeling emotionally cut off From: family, friends, or co-workers? Please describe your experiences in trying to connect with these individuals.*

_____

_____

_____

_____

_____

_____

i) *Discuss Any Loss of Interest in what you used to enjoy?*

_____

_____

_____

_____

_____

_____

j) *Do you have memory problems? There are several types of memory, which are explained and listed below. Please indicate which ones are difficult for you.*

_____

_____

_____

_____

_____

Short Term Memory – Are you able to immediately recall recent or new verbal and visual information, remembering what was just said?

_____

_____

_____

_____

_____

Recent Memory -- Can you remember new information after a time period of about 30 minutes, such as remembering the name of someone you met?

_____

_____

_____

_____

_____

Long Term Memory – Can you remember new information known previously from your work, or personal history?

_____

_____

_____

_____

_____

Procedural Memory – Can you remember a previously learned pattern such as how to turn on your computer and print information?

_____

_____

_____

_____

_____

Prospective Memory – Are you able to remember information that will be needed in the future; calling a friend, going to a doctor's appointment:

_____

_____

_____

_____

_____

k) *Avoidance – What types of things do you avoid so you are not reminded of traumatic events?*

_____

_____

_____

_____

_____

l) *Physical reactions – Do you have panic attacks or other physical reactions? Chronic pain? What parts of your body are bothering you?*

_____

_____

_____

_____

_____

m) *Flashbacks – Do your traumatic events seem to be happening again? Do you have dual awareness? (Dual awareness is the presence of mind to know where you are while you are having a flashback). Getting lost in a flashback where you believe you are actually in the location of the trauma you are reliving can be dangerous. Describe your experience during flashbacks:*

_____

_____

_____

_____

_____

n) *Do you have any dreams or nightmares about your traumatic events?*

_____

_____

_____

_____

_____

Please rate how difficult this problem is for you, with a score of 10 for very hard to 1 easy:

4. **Other Issues.**

-- *List the traumatic events in your life. List those that are most difficult for you first:*

_____

_____

_____

_____

-- Relationships: which of your relationships are healthy and supportive?

_____

_____

_____

_____

_____

-- How have you changed due to trauma? Are there adjustments you have to make because of the traumas?

_____

_____

_____

_____

_____

-- How have you coped so far? What helps? What makes life more difficult for you?

_____

_____

_____

_____

_____

_____

-- What is important for you in a therapeutic relationship?

_____

_____

_____

_____

_____

-- Do you have any problems with substance abuse? Please list the substances and how long you have been using them. Often traumatized individuals self medicate rather than seeking psychotropic medications from their PCP or a psychiatrist, which could be more helpful.

_____

_____

_____

_____

_____

-- What is your plan for dealing with PTSD? Think of who you can talk to, what you want to read, how you can care for your body. Would you consider acupuncture or massage?

_____

_____

_____

_____

_____

-- Where will you find inspiration to keep working and getting better? Remember healing can be a long process. List what you are going to do for: a. Your body, b. Your mind, c. Your spirit.

_____

_____

_____

_____

_____

_____

_____

a) *Body: Include things like exercise, massage etc.*

_____

_____

_____

_____

_____

b) *Mind: Include things like seeing your therapist, reading therapeutic materials etc.*

_____

_____

_____

_____

_____

_____

c) *Spirit: Include things that inspire you like attending AA or NA or your church or synagogue:*

_____

_____

_____

_____

_____

-- Positive Self-talk. Here are some examples of positive self-talk. Write some additional ones for yourself:

_____

_____

_____

_____

_____

-- I am healthy, prosperous, content and peaceful.

-- I am guided at every step in my healing process.

-- This too shall pass.

_____

_____

_____

_____

_____

CHAPTER 3

TREATMENT

I used DBT (Dialectical Behavioral Therapy) including things like distress tolerance skills, and mindfulness skills which were developed by Marsha Linehan, Ph.D. The therapeutic techniques came from her Skills Training Manual for Treating Borderline Personality Disorder (1993). She developed them from meditative practices in the East, especially Zen, and Western contemplative practices. Linehan initiated the use of DBT, originally for borderline personality disorder, but now it is used for many other diagnoses. Others expanded her work on mindfulness, a component of DBT, to treat many other illnesses. Here are some additional books by treatment professionals who expanded on her original work: The Mindfulness & Acceptance Workbook for Depression: Using Acceptance & Commitment Therapy to Move Through Depression & Create A Life Worth Living (2008) by Strosahl, and Robinson; and, Mindfulness & Acceptance: Expanding the Cognitive-Behavioral Tradition (2004) by Hayes, Follette and Linehan.

Coping Skills For Victims of Trauma

Coping skills are important for those with traumatic issues. Deep breathing brings oxygen to the brain and automatically helps a person reduce anxiety. To ground yourself, focus on all your senses: the sound of a fan, the sight of the sky, the taste of a lozenge, and, your body in a chair for the sense of touch. Also work at staying in the present moment, and emptying your mind of worries from the past or the future. Few of us live in the present moment, and a racing mind is exhausting. Of course your mind, just like your body, needs training, so creating a calm mind will also take time.

Imagine a peaceful beautiful place and visit it in your mind. A favorite beach, hiking area in the mountains, fishing or hunting spot, works well. Again, tune into all your senses -- the water on the beach, the breeze, the sand you're walking on, the birds singing, the trees, the sunset. The practice of using coping skills on a daily basis will become a habit and make the skills your own; thus, more accessible to you when a really bad day comes along. If you're used to using coping skills daily, or several times a day, they will be there when you really need them -- on one of those days when you get really upset. Remember how long it took you to learn the skills you use at work, so it will be worth your while to put some effort into learning coping skills.

Are there times when you are upset for a few hours or even days about how someone has treated you? Do you obsess over a slight from a family member, or a community person when driving, or your kids' behavior? It may be good to detach from a wrong done to you, because it saves you. Here are some suggestions that may require a change in your thinking, but will give you more peace. Say to yourself before you start getting really upset:

"I am peaceful. I am calm. This too shall pass."

"I can be peaceful rather than stress over this."

"I want more peace in my life, so I will think about life as it is, and not insist on how I think it should be."

Most of us do not even realize that we have expectations about how others should behave, even people we don't know. Life can be calmer and more peaceful, but it may require that we change our thinking and it will require us to stop and think before we react.

After soldiers were stable enough and were using their DBT coping skills, we started using EMDR, Eye Movement Desensitization and Reprocessing, a well researched treatment for Posttraumatic Stress Disorder, developed by Francine Shapiro, Ph.D. and described in the updated edition of her book, EMDR: The Breakthrough Therapy for Overcoming Anxiety, Stress, and Trauma (1997). EMDR has been empirically validated through 24 randomized studies, and is helpful for those with PTSD from whatever origin. If you wish to add this skill to your treatment techniques, go on line to www.emdr.com for more information, including reports of the research on this treatment technique and locations for trainings. I have found it invaluable in healing PTSD. I will give you a very short summary of how it works, but for full details visit her website, attend a training, or find a list of a therapist trained in EMDR living near you. Dr. Shapiro said:

EMDR sessions ask the client to concentrate on a disturbing part of the memory, and then let their mind move to "whatever comes up" during sets of eye movements or other forms of bilateral stimulation [such as hand taps or audio tones]...EMDR is not simple "eye movement therapy." It is a complex approach to psychotherapy that is listed in psychological encyclopedias along with psychodynamic therapy, cognitive therapy, family therapy, and so forth...EMDR addresses the emotions, thoughts, physical sensations, attitudes, behaviors, and more. Many neurologists have argued that the taps and tones work on the same principle as the eye movements, by causing an "orienting" or "interest" response in the brain that fosters the processing. Others say that the different stimuli affect the "visuo-spatial template of "working memory" (1997, Pp. xix-xx).

Advice For Trauma Victims Whose Bodies Are Now More Sensitive

For some trauma victims too much activity, light, noise, or long days can be hard to handle. This is especially true if you have Traumatic Brain Injury, an injury soldiers, domestic violence victims, those in car accidents, and other disasters share. It may be important for you to change your lifestyle by: limiting the amount of TV you watch; staying away from loud noise as much as possible; and, shortening those busy days without breaks. You may have changed since your injury and need to focus on what works best for you now. Do you feel strongest in the morning? Then, try to schedule things early, with lighter activity in the afternoon. You may not be able to do as much as you used to do. This is especially true when you are recovering physically as well as mentally. At the same time, learning some coping skills can help. Elaine Aron in her book, The Highly Sensitive Person's Workbook (1991) provides a lot of good treatment techniques about dealing with sensitivity. You might take Dr. Aron's sensitivity test to see where you are most sensitive to external stimuli. You will then become aware of the external stimuli in your life that can overwhelm you. The 4th of July fireworks, for example, can be fun for most people but soldiers after deployments can find them very hard to handle. Another good resource is Dr. Norman Doige's book, The Brain That Changes Itself: Stories of Personal Triumph from the Frontiers of Brain Science (2007). It provides inspiration for those with TBI, Traumatic Brain Injury, although it is quite technical.

The East-West Connection In Treatment Techniques

I graduated from the University of Colorado twice with bachelors and masters degrees and worked for many years writing grants funding non-profit programs. They included: programs for the homeless, a Children's Clinic, a new Girls Club, and a literacy grant for public education. Along with grant writing there were all kinds of special events I organized. Then my focus changed to clinical work, and I earned a Ph.D. in Clinical Psychology at Saybrook Institute in San Francisco. I loved the school, which included coursework from the humanistic psychologists including Abraham Maslow and his wonderful focus on psychological health.

As I have worked in different settings it became clear that the Eastern spiritual approach has also enhanced our Western treatment modalities. DBT Dialectical Behavioral Therapy by Linehan (1993), discussed earlier, was used extensively at the state hospital where I worked in Colorado and I received training in DBT there. I worked in forensics with the chronically mentally ill and in a high security unit with men who came from the prisons and we used DBT in the group treatment with them.

DBT teaches Mindfulness, which is mentioned by many of those writing in the treatment fields on depression, anxiety, substance abuse and other areas now. Marsha Linehan, Ph.D., the creator of DBT, drew from meditation practices in the East, especially from Zen, and from Western contemplative practices to create DBT. DBT includes the 3 states of mind -- Emotional, Reasonable and Wise Mind. Emotional Mind is about feelings, and Reasonable Mind is about thinking. Wise Mind combines the two plus adds intuition, logical analysis, and spiritual elements. "Mindfulness skills," according to Linehan, "are the vehicles for balancing Emotion Mind and Reasonable Mind and to achieve Wise Mind" (1993, p. 63).

Linehan further explains:

The person is in Emotional Mind when her thinking and behavior are controlled primarily by her current emotional state. In Emotional Mind cognitions are hot; reasonable logical thinking is difficult; facts are amplified or distorted to be congruent with current affect…Wise Mind is the integration of Emotional and Reasonable Mind…

It also goes beyond them: Wise Mind adds intuitive knowing to emotional experiencing and logical analysis (1993, p. 84).

DBT skills include a nonjudgmental approach to life and teaching skill building, especially distress tolerance. Meditative techniques and self-soothing practices such as prayer, and imagery, are part of the skills, as well. They are called Crisis Survival Strategies and they awaken those traumatized to the body-mind-spirit connection. When running groups at the state hospital, I would bring in snacks and we would watch a video of the majestic Grand Canyon with Tangerine Dream music. The prisoners were learning self-care and relaxation skills; something with which most of them had no previous experience. I asked a roomful of these men once about their experiences growing up specifically, when had they left home? Almost all of them had been thrown out of or lost their homes in their early teen years. It is difficult if not impossible to survive on the street at 13 without getting into trouble, and obviously they had gotten into trouble.

With DBT's teachings of the 3 states of mind-- Emotional, Reasonable and Wise Mind, the prisoners were helped to move from a focus on emotions, and impulsive acts to being more reasonable and wise in their actions. Wise Mind had a spiritual component, as well. DBT treatment was based on body-mind-spirit principles and I felt it was very helpful for them. After this treatment was developed there have been multiple books out on Mindfulness and it is well accepted in the treatment field. Treatment is no longer based on just the medical model. Some additional books on Mindfulness include: <u>The Mindfulness & Acceptance Workbook for Depression</u> (2008) by Kirk D. Stosahl, Ph.D. and Patricia J. Robinson Ph.D., and, <u>The Dialectical Behavioral Therapy Skills Workbook for Bipolar Disorder: Using DBT To Regain Control of Your Emotions and Your Life</u> (2009) by Rebecca E. Williams and Julie S. Kraft MA. The addition of Eastern thought has strengthened the treatment practices for Western providers and patients.

Body-Mind-Spirit Connection

What is that unique contribution you can make; that only you can make? Don't fool yourself. It is important. We are all unique. You are one of those links in a long chain of humans -- pass on to the next generation your finest contributions. I believe

35

we get lost in daily survival, so lest we forget, we don't have forever here. We are all just passing through. If you need guidance and protection, ask the spirit, your higher power, God, the universe, to help you. All you need to do is ask.

Understand that there is a strong connection between your body, mind and spirit. A wound to any side of the triangle affects all three sides. Any time you work on one of the sides of this triangle you improve the other two sides, as well. So, massage, meditation, taking a class to educate yourself, visiting your doctor, eating healthy, seeing your therapist, all these things help the body, the mind, and the spirit.

Working in the trauma field requires constant work on oneself to be able to provide guidance on the problems that patients bring to you. For inspiration, I have read Dr. Wayne Dyer's book, There's a Spiritual Solution to Every Problem (2001) over and over again. I would forget my connection to spirit and this book would bring me back in touch with spirit, where I could see there really was no problem spirit could not solve, if you remembered to ask for help and get your ego out of the way. It seems that inspiration is a requirement for all of us and especially for those in the helping professions.

Things are changing regarding medications for PTSD. Due to the many overdoses and deaths with benzodiazepines and opioids, once freely used to treat anxiety and panic attacks, medication providers are very careful now in prescribing them. Too many individuals have overdosed by mixing them with street drugs and alcohol. If you have difficulty getting meds that work for you there are other options. I recommend the advice in Bourne, Brownstein and Garano's book, Natural Relief for Anxiety: Complementary strategies for Easing Fear, Panic & Worry (2004).

Good Self-Care For Victims of Trauma

A major issue for all those with PTSD is learning good self-care. Service Members are trained to take care of each other, especially those in roles of authority. They respond to their cell phones 24/7. They give a lot and often do not think very much about themselves. They can have very demanding jobs. They are dedicated individuals. They can burn out if they are not aware of how to take care of themself, especially after several deployments. Domestic violence victims can also neglect their health, have injuries from severe abuse by their partner, and lack the financial means to obtain good self-care. A stay in a domestic violence shelter can change all that and initiate a new life. To find a domestic violence shelter near you and the community programs the shelter offers check Appendix A and call the National Domestic Violence Hotline. They maintain up to date information about all the domestic violence programs around the country.

All survivors of PTSD need to pay special attention to issues like sleep. For soldier's, specifically, long hours during deployments and lack of sleep, can set them on a new pattern that can continue after they come home. They may have slept with one eye open, and that feeling of needing to be alert to danger -- hyper-vigilance, can be hard to shake. Domestic violence and sexual abuse victims can have the same issue. At the shelter where I worked in Boulder, victims were aware of every car that drove by them while they were walking out in the community and feared being followed. The stay at the shelter may be the first time they have slept well in months or years. Sexual abuse victims abused while they slept can have life long sleep issues as well.

Home can feel more dangerous than it did before a soldier deployed. They have survived due to their watchfulness and vigilance, and that skill is part of their training. They will not be able to flip a switch and shut off this valuable skill very easily, now that they are home. Their perception of danger has increased. Things they may not have worried about at home before deploying may seem much more threatening to them now. Hyper vigilance is one of the symptoms of trauma. Those in car accidents may have a hard time driving after a bad accident; rape victims may fear going out alone even to safe areas. Trauma changes our perceptions of danger, and our bodies react as well. Noise, crowds, going through intersections, and drivers who are inappropriate, may elicit anger and feelings of danger. Although soldiers may intellectually realize they are home, their body and their mind may need some time to adjust. The same can be said for all PTSD survivors. Your body has learned to become alert and aware of everything happening around you and that skill is how you survived. Relaxing your body now will take some time and some new skills.

Finding a Psychologist for Treatment

Each state has a Psychological Association. Call their office and request the names of several psychologists with expertise in trauma work. I would recommend training in EMDR. Give them the name of your insurance and your location. They will call you back with the names of several providers that can meet your needs. Then make some calls and decide whom you want to work with. If you end up with someone who is not a good fit do not hesitate to try another provider.

Reporting Abuse

Each county in the United States has a Department of Human Services with a child and adult protective services unit. Any abuse of a child or senior citizen can be reported to them and they will investigate it. It can be done anonymously.

CHAPTER 4

RESILIENCY

Resiliency is the psychological equivalent of physical stamina. With resilience you can get through things, you can persevere. We each have our own style and ways of being resilient, but if you have gone through lots of trauma and are still functioning you have it. Be generous in your self-praise. Only you know what you have been through and how you survived, but, you have survived and that is the key. Al Siebert, Ph.D. is an expert in this area, and has written several books especially helpful for soldiers. They include: <u>The Resiliency Advantage: Master Change, Thrive Under Pressure, and Bounce Back From Setbacks</u> (2005), and, <u>The Survivor Personality: Why Some People Are Stronger, Smarter, and More Skillful at Handling Life's Difficulties … and How You Can Be, Too</u> (1993).

The experts say highly resilient people can adapt to change. They look for the opportunities in changing circumstances. And, they do all this while staying healthy, learning to work in new ways, and without falling into bad habits or dysfunctional responses to stress.

Here are a few pointers for trauma victims as they go through treatment. Remember to congratulate yourself! You must have been a resilient person to have survived and functioned so well for so many years with all you have experienced. The following are some additional suggestions to strengthen your resiliency.

Calmness

Calmness is a learned response. Deep breathe. Find time to meditate. Walk or run. Talk to a peaceful friend. Think of the big picture. Tell yourself this too shall pass.

Learn Problem Solving Skills

Problem solving incudes these steps: 1.) Get input from those involved, analyze the situation and state the facts; 2.) Have those involved think of several options to solve the problem and allow brain- storming where solutions are given but not analyzed or ruled out at this point. Even what may seem like crazy ideas are written down; 3.) Have those involved state the pros and cons to the solutions; 4.) Decide on a solution to try and revisit the issue in a certain amount of time to see how it is working.

Humor

Neuropsychologists tell us there are two ways to change our behavior. As we often do, we start down the well-worn path trying the same old thing, and then have to back up and create a new path. Or, we can use humor and jump out of that old path more quickly and less painfully, to try something new. No wonder we love the clowns and jesters of the world. Laughter is very healthy, as is seeing the funny side of a situation. Edward DeBono in his book, DeBono's Thinking Course (1982) tells us: "In terms of mind, the mechanisms for pattern changing are mistake, accident, and humor…Humor is probably the most significant characteristic of the human mind…But humor can only occur in a self-organizing patterning system of the sort we find in human perception. Humor involves the escape from the pattern and the switching into another" (p. 55).

See Yourself As Unique

Describe yourself in the highest and most positive terms possible, especially to yourself. Positive self-talk helps, such as: I can do this. I will take my time and conquer this. Every day I am getting stronger.

Flexibility

Having options is vital in changing times. If you can't think of any find a life coach or good friend and brainstorm with this person.

Life-Long Learning

You'll still be 50 whether you start working on that degree or not. Why not start now and increase your options of being able to find a new job.

World Views

How do you see the world? What has changed for you? Are you fighting these changes? Try a new approach. Embrace the changes and see what new thoughts you have.

Read Some History & Check Out Resources

History will give you newfound respect for leaders that have dealt with the impossible such as wars and depressions, and, help put your own issues in perspective. See Appendix A. for a list of resources for those with trauma including books, and websites.

Ancient Teachings

Psychologist Wayne Dyer, in his book, "Change Your Thoughts – Change Your Life: Living the Wisdom of the Tao," provides a modern interpretation of an ancient Chinese text, 25 centuries old, the Tao Te Ching, or the Great Way. Dyer says, "It offers advice, and guidance that is balanced, moral, spiritual and always concerned with working for the good." The Tao Te Ching emphasizes the natural world and it is relaxing and inspiring to read, and something that still applies now after so many centuries. It also does a pretty good job about reducing the fear most of us have about death. Some of my severely injured car accident patients have read it and they experienced a reduction in anxiety and worry as their cases proceeded through a period of difficult court proceedings.

CHAPTER 5

PREVENTION

First You Must Survive

If you want a long life, there are things that you want to do, and things you do not want to do. As I have seen thousands of people for disability assessments, all this has become very clear to me. I see all kinds of physical and mental heath problems. You might say, I have become highly sensitized to what individuals do to their bodes; and, the things that happen as a result of trauma, disease, accidents, and, bad habits, that can have repercussions for a life time. All these issues may produce PTSD symptoms as well.

As much as possible we can prevent problems and improve our future by taking action. Also we can strengthen our lives by what we do not do. Prevention requires handling one's impulsivity for the sake of keeping one's body safe. We get only one body and, the body you start out with is the one you are stuck with to the end of your days. Make your body a place you want to live in. The following lists some common sense bits of advice.

Smoking

When you are young it may seem harmless to smoke, but over time it can become an addiction and shorten your life. It is easy to get into something but extremely hard to get out of it, and smoking fits this description. I have seen patients follow in their parents' footsteps. The parents have died of lung cancer and the adult children continue to smoke for 25 years, seemingly in an unconscious fashion, repeating the fate of their parents. Many times they seem to be surprised when they become ill. It seems that they are in denial about their addiction and did not think about the long-term outcome of their behavior. Anything we grow up with seems normal to us, even the bad habits of our relatives.

I've had patients come in with terminal diagnoses due to cigarettes, expressing a lot of anger, and, blaming the environment, instead of their smoking, for their illnesses. I've also had young patients tell me about growing up with chain smoking parents who affected their lives due to all the chemical exposure they had growing up. They were living with the unconscious behavior of their parents.

Smoking, according to everything I have seen, is the most difficult addiction to kick, perhaps only second to meth addiction. It is definitely something that can shorten your life and hauling around oxygen tanks in your senior years is not fun either. This is something definitely to avoid.

Food

In Hawaii, diabetes is common and there is an active promotion to have young people limit their intake of pop/soda, which is full of sugar. A parent can help by limiting a child's access to sugar drinks and thus help them develop good eating habits. The national issue of obesity also is partially due to sugar drinks, so this is also another result of poor eating habits. Again, changing one's habits to drinking water instead of sugar drinks will help you keep your weight down and, hopefully, prevent you from having to deal with diabetes.

Safety

Accidents of all types can have long-term affects on your life. When driving, biking, riding on a scooter in traffic, or surfing in the ocean, be aware of things around you. Of course, all accidents cannot be prevented, but know your risks when you take up a sport, drive in bad weather, or on a bicycle in traffic.

Drugs & Alcohol

I have worked with many families who have patterns regarding drug and alcohol use. Use often begins early just like smoking. Drug and alcohol use often coincides with school problems and perhaps dropping out of school. If you take a history from an adult they often tell you when they quit school, and then later if you ask them when they started using drugs of alcohol, it coincides with when they stopped going to school. So, parents have to be vigilant with their children. If children and adolescents are using when young, this is a major indication of problems that can interfere with success in many areas of life later on.

Basic Skills

Learning basic skills like multiplication tables, and reading are very important for basic functioning. It is amazing how many adults do not know their multiplication tables, or basic historical information about our culture. Homework teaches children to complete work and turn it in. It is preparation for work life. Make sure your children develop this habit. Reading is an acquired taste, so reading to your children when they are young helps develop this taste. Get them hooked into reading. Find out what they are interested in and read books on these topics to them.

Paying Attention

Do your children have an unusual insect bite? I recently met with a patient who told me a story about her youth in which her step mother did not pick up on a bite she got on her face which developed into Lyme's disease and because it was not found for 5 years, was already at the stage 3 level and hard to deal with. Catch things early and pay close attention to your children and significant others. If your child is having trouble in school, ask for an assessment so they can obtain additional help. Do not let things slide. Do not let your child get discouraged. Taking action is important and can prevent long-term problems.

Motivation & Education

Do everything you can to become as well educated as you can. Go for additional training, go back to school for another degree. Don't let age stop you. Don't give up. If you love a particular subject or area of interest that may be the area you may want to pursue.

Work

It is best to find work you enjoy or even love. It can take time to find it so don't give up. I went back to school for my doctorate later in life and feel that if I had not I would probably have been laid off. I also love my work and hope to be doing it for a long time into the future. I have been able to change the populations and locations I work in and that has kept me interested since I am always learning new things.

Awareness

We often are shocked by what goes unnoticed in the world. Be a person who stands up for something. Report things you see that seem illegal or unhealthy. Your awareness can help protect the more vulnerable in our society. It also helps prevent trauma from developing so victims don't spend years dealing with abuse.

The Universe, God, Jesus, Buddha, Higher Power

In working with many, many people, I can say those with a spiritual or religious orientation of some kind, seem to do better in a crisis. Just even understanding you are a part of the Universe is helpful. The feeling of connection to something greater than one's individual life, of 100 years or so, is important. The soldiers I worked with who could lean on their faith recovered better and found more meaning in their lives. This brings us back to the body-mind-spirit connection again. Put some time into each side of the triangle to strengthen yourself.

Owning Your Own Power

What can you do to improve your life and happiness? A little girl I worked with talked to a police officer she saw about abuse that was happening to her in her home, and, was told how to report it. She reported it and it stopped. She took matters into her own hands and improved her life. There is help if you need to leave a domestic violence situation, or if you need to go back to school to improve your chances of getting a job, or, if you need to move somewhere where there are more job opportunities.

Change

The familiar is comfortable. Change is scary. How does one work with change? You might start by trying something new, visiting a new location, or asking questions of those who have made a lot of changes and find out how they did it. Transitions can be planned so a change does not feel so bad. If you end up having to move for a better opportunity, plan to visit the family you have left behind several times a year, for instance, to prevent homesickness.

With change, know there is always fear involved. Natural changes like aging, leaving home after high school, marriage, divorce, job changes, changes in relationships, death of parents, changes in financial status, all can cause fear. But, the only things we can count on is that there will always be change. Talking it out with someone can help.

Talking It Out

Find someone, or pay someone, to talk to when life becomes difficult. If you are impulsive, acting from feelings without thinking of the consequences, can be dangerous. Impulsivity is a characteristic of those who end up in jail or prison during their lives, and I have worked with many such individuals. It is best to talk to someone to broaden your options. Don't take that drastic action. Talk to someone first.

Relationships

Relationship issues are complicated by PTSD and can be at the heart of one's concerns when domestic violence is involved. The best advice I have read regarding healthy relationships comes from John Gottman, Ph.D., author of, <u>The Seven Principles for Making Marriage Work</u> (1999). He emphasizes the importance of friendship in successful marriages and relationships. Friendship is the skill that keeps things working and makes life together pleasant and worthwhile. If you are working to improve a relationship, or starting over with a new relationship, building a friendship helps create a solid foundation for any new or renewed relationship. We often treat our friends much better than our partners.

It really matters whom you associate with. Are the people you are thinking of spending time with healthy, law abiding, and happy? They will influence your life. Does the guy/gal you're thinking of dating have a scary side? Do they appear to have untreated mental health problems? Are you a means to an end? Is there a balance in the relationship? We are often attracted to those who are very different, new or novel, but will this end badly? What are the risks?

Dr. Gabor Mate in his book, <u>When the Body Says No: Exploring the Stress-Disease Connection</u> (2003) tells the stories of countless patients he has seen who were more prone to all kinds of illnesses due to early abuse and lack of self care. And, he discovered that these issues are passed down through the generations. It is important not to pass down any abuse you have experienced; to be the one who stops the abuse. It is best to pass on only the best of yourself and, in addition, to passing on an openness and interest to healing any wounds you may have.

CHAPTER 6

INSPIRATION

How does one stay inspired? This is an especially important question for those who are working through trauma issues and for those working with them in the helping professions. Working with trauma can be energy draining, and you can forget your connection to the universe, to your higher power, and, to the big picture. We all can lose touch with those people and things that inspire us and keep us going. Here is a meditation I use that inspires me:

The Meditation for the World

Imagine yourself in the universe, surrounded by the stars, and looking at the beautiful blue earth. You are holding hands with all the people around the globe. You are all surrounding the earth looking down on it and the stars are all around you. As all the people on the earth circle the globe, behind each of these people in a long line is everyone from their family that came before them, all their ancestors. You turn and thank your ancestors for everything they did for you. In front of you are those coming after you, the future generations -- bless them.

Now send your love around the circle to all those alive on the earth today. All of humanity is with you in the meditation, everyone who has ever lived, everyone who is alive now, and, everyone who is ever going to live. You send peace and love around the circle and it flows through the hands of all those alive today, all those who have ever live, and all those who will live after you in the future. You are experiencing in this meditation the fellowship of the human spirit. If all the bad news happening around the world can be broadcast each day, then good news can also be broadcast. It is time to see in a new way. Each individual holding hands around the circle is a soul, each one of us will live and die on this planet. We have similar experiences through our lifetimes. We are all connected. We can send blessings to each other, along with feelings of peace and love.

We are all one in spirit. All the ideas that have propelled us forward are still part of all of those on the earth today. We all benefit from the brilliance of those that came before us. We are in that lineup of those who came before us and those coming after us. We know we will, very soon, be ancestors ourselves.

Our Ancestors

We bowed to our ancestors in the Meditation to the World, and what follows are some examples of those who listened to their destiny call and answered that calling for the benefit of all those who came after them.

John Adams, our second president, and his wife Abigail endured years apart as the U.S. was being born. So did George Washington and his wife Martha. They were thinking of future generations when they created this country. We owe them a lot.

More personally, my great grandfather built roads where there were none and a beautiful church, the first in a rural community in Minnesota. I spent many hours in that church. I did not find out how instrumental my great grandfather was in building it for many years. You matter a lot to everyone around you. You are one person in a long chain that will continue on into the future. We are all connected. To feel this connection as you did in the Meditation For the World is to see the value of your life in a different way. It is to honor your spiritual side.

This is just a tiny taste of what all of us enjoy because of the hard work and dedication of those that came before us. There are advocates serving the human spirit all over the world from all times. We can be so focused on our own 75 or 100 years of human life on the planet that we lose the big picture. To focus on the big picture means to think about those who came before us and those who will come after us. It is to be aware of our mortality.

Gratitude

Gratitude lifts us up and fills our hearts. We all contribute in our own way just by loving our own families and thinking of the elderly -- those before us, and the children -- those coming after us. To make their lives happy and delightful is a great contribution to emotional health that will be felt down through the generations. This is no small thing. I see those who suffer for years from early abuse in childhood and adolescence in my work as a psychologist.

Currently, gratitude is a big issue in mental health circles. In his book, <u>The Power of Intention: Learning to Co-Create Your World Your Way</u> (2004) Dr. Dyer tells us: "Stay in gratitude. This is the surest way to keep the connecting link to perfect health clean and pure" (p. 229). You can do this by starting off your day by thanking the Universe for all you have. Gratitude continues to attract more good into your life. Call on your higher power, Spirit, God, each morning to guide and protect you. Hand over any issues you need help with to this higher power. You must ask for help. Since we all have free will, your higher power, God, the angels, your guru, must all be invited in and this may require setting up reminders to yourself. I have one in my car that says, "protection on?" Why try to handle all life's challenges alone when you can call on help? Check out this website on gratitude: <u>www.gratefulness</u>.org.

Renewing One's Energy

It is easy to get lost in the day-to-day details of life; to lose one's connection to the spirit; to get tired; to lose one's focus. Clarisa Pinkola Estes, a Jungian analyst, in her book, <u>Women Who Run With the Wolves: Myths and Stories of the Wild Woman Archetype</u> (1992), taught that stories were medicine. In the story, "The Three Golden Hairs" (Pp. 328 – 333), she relates that if we have been working hard on something there will come a time when we will become completely worn out. At such a time, we need to rock ourselves back to health to "renew the creative fire", to restore ourselves. This often means taking a break. Estes says, "To lose focus means to lose energy. The absolutely wrong thing to do is to attempt to rush about struggling to pack it all back together again. Rushing is not the thing to do…sitting and rocking is the thing to do."(1992, p. 329). How important it is to have the presence of mind to slow down and rock.

Another great author, Elaine Aron, Ph.D., focuses on our ability to renew our creative fire by honoring our sensitivity, in her book, <u>The Highly Sensitive Person's Workbook</u> (1990). This book was a great help to the soldiers I worked with. PTSD had made them very sensitive to stimulation from the outside world. The 4th of July was a nightmare for them. All that noise sounded like gunfire and they would come in very distressed after dealing with their flashbacks. This book provides prescriptions on how to take care of your sensitivity in a world of noise and communication overload.

Mythology

Estes and Aron's books have been medicine, ancient medicine, and they are international. Estes found similar stories all over the world in many different cultures. Joseph Campbell said it too, in <u>The Hero With a Thousand Faces</u> (1949). For Campbell, the mythologies from all over the world told a similar story, and he saw them as just one song. Campbell's field was Comparative Mythology and he found similar themes in all the myths. The hero theme was in all cultures and the journey the hero traveled was a familiar path. In the hero, Campbell had found a universal theme. Carl Jung also saw the connection we all had as well, in his concept of the collective unconscious. He saw that we were all connected at an unconscious level.

The Fellowship of the Human Spirit

Over the archway of the University of Colorado library in Boulder are the words: "Enter here the fellowship of the human spirit." I read these words while a student at CU and felt that it was a privilege to explore the great thoughts and ideas of those who had gone before me. To enter the fellowship of the human spirit -- how could one ask more of life than that?

Many scientists thought that our consciousness expanded when we landed on the moon and saw the earth for the first time from that vantage point. We became aware of our home in a whole new way. It is important for us to stay connected with others around the world. In Estes's story, "Seal Skin, Soul Skin," the seal mother tells her son to just "touch my things, my firesticks, my stone carvings and I will be with you always." (1992, p. 290).

If we all practiced the Meditation for the World we might remember how connected we all are on this earth and how many of us are working to improve the world. Let us focus on the good that is happening, and, there is a lot of good happening all around us.

CHAPTER 7

RECENT RESEARCH ON TRAUMA TREATMENTS

Meditation

The Neuropsychological research field has come up with new treatments for trauma including Meditation, and walking. Jennifer Sweeton, Psy.D in her book "Trauma Treatment Toolbox" (2019), describes the benefits for the brain with meditation including…"less activation of the fear center, the amygdala…that reduces reactions to trauma triggers, reduces stress responses, and increases the relaxation response and decreases hyper-vigilance." Meditation also, "increases the feelings of safety… in the hippocampus" and, "reduces fear when faced with trauma triggers." Meditation "activates the thinking center of the brain, the prefrontal cortex," and helps a trauma victim "think more clearly, make better decisions, and assists with concentration and attention." Meditation also assists the "self-regulation center of the brain, the cingulate, assisting with regulation of the emotions, and the management of any distressing thoughts."p.165-166. In general, meditation, according to Sweeton, assists in the integration and communication between brain centers. I've had patients tell me they notice they function better if they meditate before doing homework or taking tests and it clears up distress.

Walking & Yoga

In his book, "In Praise of Walking: A New Scientific Exploration" (2019) Dr. O'Mara through his research tells us walking helps our thinking, our mood, repairs organs, keeps our brains from aging, protects the heart, and produces new cells in the hippocampus which is involved with learning and memory. O'Mara encourages us to have regular contact with nature as it helps restore us. Yoga is also recommended as good treatment for trauma and there are many websites such as www.yogainternational.com, which are reasonable for on-line training.

I wish you great success in all your healing efforts! Dr. C.

REFERENCES

Aron, Elaine N. (1999). The highly sensitive person's workbook. New York, NY: Random House.

Beck, A. T. (1993). BAI Beck anxiety inventory. San Antonio, Texas: Pearson Clinical Assessment.

Beck, A. T., Steer, R. A., & Brown, G. K. (1996) BDI-II Beck depression inventory, II. San Antonio, Texas: Pearson Psychological Assessment.

Bourne, Edmund J., Brownstein, A. & Garano, Lorna (2004). Natural relief for anxiety: Complementary strategies for easing fear, panic & worry. Oakland, CA: New Harbinger Publications, Inc.

Briere, J. (1989). Therapy for adults molested as children: Beyond survival. New York, NY: Springer Publishing Company, Inc.

Briere, J. (1991). TSI Trauma symptom inventory. Lutz, Florida: PAR, Inc.

Campbell, J. (1949) The hero with a thousand faces. Princeton, N J: Princeton University Press.

Cosineau, P. & Brown, S. (1990). The hero's journey: Joseph

Campbell on his life and work. New York, NY: Harper & Row Publishers.

DeBono, E. (1982). DeBono's thinking course. New York, NY: Facts On File, Inc.

Desk Reference to the Diagnostic Criteria from DSM-5. (2013). Arlington, VA: American Psychiatric Association.

Doidge, N. (2007). <u>The bran that changes itself: Stories of personal triumph from the frontiers of brain science</u>. New York, NY: The Penguin Group.

Dyer, W. W. (2007) <u>Change your thoughts – Change your life: Living the wisdom of the Tao</u>. Carlsbad, CA: Hay House, Inc.

Dyer, W. W. (2004). <u>The power of intention: Learning to co-create your world your way</u>. Carlsbad, CA: Hay House, Inc.

Dyer, W. W. (2001). <u>There's a spiritual solution to every problem</u>. New York, NY: HarperCollins Publishers.

Estes, C. P. (1992). <u>Women who run with the wolves: Myths and stories of the wild woman archetype</u>. New York, NY: Random House.

Gabor M. (2003). <u>When the body says no: Exploring the stress-disease connection.</u> Hoboken New Jersey, John Wiley & Sons.

Hindman, J. (1989). <u>Just before dawn: From the shadows of tradition to new reflections in trauma assessment and treatment of sexual victimization.</u> Ontario, Oregon: AlexAndria Associates.

Hayes, S. C., Follette, V. M. & Linehan, M. M. (2004). <u>Mindfulness and acceptance: Expanding the cognitive-behavioral tradition</u>. New York, NY: The Guilford Press.

Linehan, M. M. (1993) <u>Skills training manual for treating borderline personality disorder</u>. New York, NY: The Guilford Press.

Mate, G. (2003). <u>When the body says no: Exploring the stress-disease connection</u>. Hoboken, New Jersey: John Wiley & Sons, Inc.

O'Mara, Shane (2019) <u>In praise of walking: A new scientific exploration.</u> New York, NY: The Random House Group Ltd.

Rubin, G. (2009). <u>The happiness project</u>. New York, NY: HarperCollins.

Shapiro, F. & Forrest, Margot S. (1997). <u>EMDR: The breakthrough therapy for overcoming anxiety, stress, and trauma.</u> New York, NY: Perseus Book Group.

Siebert, A. (1993). <u>The survivor personality: Why some people are stronger, smarter, and more skillful at handling life's difficulties and how you can be, too.</u> New York, NY: Pedigree Books.

Siebert, A. (2005). <u>The resiliency advantage: Master change, thrive under pressure, and bounce back from setbacks.</u> San Francisco, CA: Berrett-Koehler Publishers, Inc.

Strosahl K. D. & Robinson, P. J. (2008). <u>The mindfulness & acceptance workbook for depression: Using acceptance & commitment therapy to move through depression & create a life worth living.</u> Oakland, CA: New Harbinger Publications, Inc.

Sweeton, Jennifer. (2019). <u>Trauma Treatment Toolbox: 165 brain-challenging tips, tools & handouts to move therapy forward.</u> Eau Claire, WI: PESI Publishing & Media.

Van Gijk, S. (2009). <u>The dialectical behavioral therapy skills workbook for bipolar disorder: Using DBT to regain control of your emotions and your life.</u> Oakland, CA: New Harbinger Publications, Inc.

Weathers, Litz, Huska & Keane (1994) <u>PCL-M for DSM-IV.</u>

Desk Reference to the Diagnostic Criteria from DSM-5. Honolulu, HI: National Center for PTSD-Behavioral Science Division.

A P P E N D I X A

Resources

Books

Aaron, Elaine, N. (1999). The Highly Sensitive Person's Workbook. New York, NY: Random House.

Doidge, Norman, M.D. (2007). The Brain That Changes Itself: Stories of Personal Triumph from the frontiers of Brain Science. New York, NY: The Penguin Group.

Dyer, Wayne W., Ph.D. – Any book by this author, which can be found in the Self Help sections of book stores.

Gottman, John M. Ph.D. (1999). The Seven Principles for Making Marriage Work.

Hayes, S. C., Follette, V. M. & Linhan, M. M. (2004). Mindfulness & Acceptance: Expanding the Cognitive-Behavioral Tradition. New York: NY: The Guilford Press.

Hanson, Rick, Ph.D., and Mendius, Richard, M.D. (2009). Budda's Brain: The Practical Neuroscience of Happiness, Love & Wisdom.

Love and Logic Institute, Inc. for parenting tapes, books and videos. www.loveandlogic.com. 2207 Jackson St., Golden, CO 80401.

Siebert, Al, Ph.D., (1993). The Survivor Personality: Why Some People are Stronger, Smarter, and More Skillful at Handling Life's Difficulties and How You Can Be Too. New York: NY: Pedigree Books.

Siebert, Al, Ph.D. (2005). The Resiliency Advantage: Master Chang, Thrive Under pressure, and Bounce Back From Setbacks. San Francisco, CA: Berrett-Koehler Publishers, Inc.

Strosahl, Kirk D. Ph.D. and Robinson, Patricia J. Ph.D. (2008). The Mindfulness & Acceptance Workbook for Depression: Using Acceptance & Commitment Therapy to Move Through Depression & Create a Life Worth Living. Oakland, CA: New Harbinger Publications, Inc.

PHONE NUMBERS AND WEBSITES

www.ARMYOneSource

www.militaryonesource.com 1-800-342-9647 Open 24/7

National Domestic Violence Hotline 1-800-799-7233

National Coalition Against Domestic Violence (303) 839-1852

Suicide Prevention 1-800-suicide

Wounded Soldier & Family Hotline 1-800-984-8532

www.emdr.com - For training, and full reports on research on EMDR treatment.

www.behavioraltech.com- for training in DBT.

www.gratefulness.org.

Printed in the United States
By Bookmasters